Discover Life in North Carolina: Moving to Pittsboro, Sanford, Carthage, Siler City, and Asheboro

Your Essential Relocation Guide

By Crystal Hutchinson

© 2024 Crystal Hutchinson. All rights reserved.

No part of this publication may be reproduced, distributed, or transmitted in any form or by any means, including photocopying, recording, or other electronic or mechanical methods, without the prior written permission of the publisher, except in the case of brief quotations embodied in critical reviews and certain other noncommercial uses permitted by copyright law. For permission requests, write to the publisher at the email address below.

Published by Crystal Hutchinson
Email: crystalsellsnchomes@gmail.com

First Edition: 2024

Printed in the United States of America

Table of Contents

Chapter 1: Welcome to North Carolina's Historic Heartlands......5

Chapter 2: Real Estate Market Insights 10

Chapter 3: Moving and Relocation Essentials..........16

Chapter 4: Community and Social Life........22

Chapter 5: Government and Public Services............28

Chapter 6: Education and Local Schools........35

Chapter 7: Healthcare and Emergency Services........44

Chapter 8: Parks, Recreation, and Green Living 55

Chapter 9: Economic Opportunities and Employment..........64

Chapter 10: Homebuying and Financial Planning.........72

Chapter 11: Staying Healthy During Transitions 80

Appendices:........87

About the Author........99

References 101

Preface

Welcome to your comprehensive guide to relocating to some of North Carolina's most cherished towns. Whether you're moving for a change of scenery, family, or career, the journey to a new home is exciting and, at times, daunting. This guide is designed to ease your transition, providing you with detailed insights into the real estate market, community life, and much more about Pittsboro, Sanford, Carthage, Siler City, and Asheboro.

As a licensed real estate broker and former attorney who moved to Raleigh in 2022, I have experienced firsthand the challenges and rewards of relocating. My mission is to equip you with the knowledge and tools needed to make informed decisions and find a community where you can thrive.

Let's embark on this journey together, discovering the unique charm and opportunities that North Carolina's Historic Heartlands have to offer.

Chapter 1: Welcome to North Carolina's Historic Heartlands

Introduction to the Heartlands

North Carolina's Historic Heartlands offer a tapestry of American history, culture, and community spirit. In this chapter, we journey through the towns of Pittsboro, Sanford, Carthage, Siler City, and Asheboro. Each town, with its unique heritage and distinct charm, represents an essential chapter of North Carolina's story, inviting you to be a part of its ongoing narrative.

Pittsboro: A Quaint Blend of Old and New

Founded in 1785, Pittsboro is a picturesque town that boasts a rich history and vibrant community. The historic courthouse, situated in the heart of the town square, serves as a focal point around which the community's life revolves. This town seamlessly blends the old with the new. Antique shops, local bookstores, and artisan coffee shops line the streets, housed in well-preserved buildings that date back to the early 1900s.

Pittsboro is also a hub for sustainable living and innovation, evidenced by its numerous organic farms and the presence of the Eco Industrial Park. The community is deeply committed to environmental stewardship, which aligns with the modern push towards sustainability while respecting its historical roots. The annual Pittsboro Street Fair showcases local crafts, arts, and foods, drawing visitors and locals alike into a vibrant celebration of small-town life.

Sanford: The Heartbeat of North Carolina

Established in 1874 as a railroad depot named "Jonesboro Junction," Sanford has grown into a bustling center of commerce and culture. Known as "The Heart of North Carolina," its strategic location has historically made it a gathering point for various industries. Today, Sanford's economy thrives on its rich clay deposits, which continue to support a flourishing brick and pottery industry.

Sanford's downtown area, with its historic architecture, features an array of modern boutiques, breweries, and eateries, creating a lively atmosphere that honors its historical roots. The town's cultural scene is highlighted by the annual Sanford Pottery Festival, celebrating local and national potters. For outdoor enthusiasts, the nearby Deep River offers canoeing and scenic trails, providing a natural retreat from the urban environment.

Carthage: Echoes of the Past

Carthage, the oldest town in Moore County, was settled in 1784 and has a storied history as a center for turpentine and timber production. Its historic downtown is dominated by the Moore County Courthouse, an impressive neoclassical structure built in 1922, around which the town's history revolves.

Today, Carthage is renowned for preserving its heritage while fostering a community-focused lifestyle. The Carthage Buggy Festival, a unique local event, commemorates the town's history as a once-thriving manufacturer of horse-drawn buggies. This festival not only celebrates the past but also brings the community together, with music, food, and crafts that showcase the town's enduring spirit and cultural pride.

Siler City: A Cultural Melting Pot

Siler City was established in 1884 and has evolved from a quiet railroad community to a vibrant cultural hub. Its diversity is one of its most defining characteristics, with a significant Latino population enriching the town with cultural festivals, diverse cuisine, and bilingual community programs.

Art and creativity are at the heart of Siler City, anchored by the NC Arts Incubator. This facility provides a space for artists to create and sell their work, driving cultural engagement and economic development within the community. Siler City's commitment to arts and multicultural integration makes it a unique place where different cultures coalesce, offering residents a rich, inclusive community experience.

Asheboro: Harmony with Nature

Asheboro, founded in 1796, is known for its harmonious blend of nature and urban life. Home to the North Carolina Zoo, it offers an expansive view of what it means to live in close proximity to both wildlife and city comforts. The zoo, one of the largest natural habitat zoos in the world, exemplifies the town's commitment to conservation and education.

The downtown area of Asheboro is vibrant, with local shops, galleries, and restaurants that cater to an eco-conscious community. Annual events like the Fall Festival reflect the town's spirit, combining arts, crafts, food, and entertainment. Asheboro's extensive park systems and community-focused initiatives make it an ideal place for those who value a lifestyle that balances ecological awareness with vibrant community interactions.

Conclusion: The Lure of Small-Town Life

In North Carolina's Historic Heartlands, the past is not just preserved; it is a living, breathing part of each town's present and future. These towns offer more than just a place to live—they offer a place to be a part of a continuing story. Whether it's the artistic streets of Siler City, the bustling historic downtown of Sanford, the tranquil, tree-lined avenues of Carthage, the charming blend of old and new in Pittsboro, or the nature-infused vibrancy of Asheboro, each town offers a unique slice of life. Here, you find more than a home; you find a heritage to share in and a community to grow with.

This detailed exploration invites you to experience the essence of living in each town, providing a deep understanding of what makes each location not just a dot on the map, but a place to call home.

Chapter 2: Real Estate Market Insights

Introduction to Market Dynamics

North Carolina's Historic Heartlands, encompassing Pittsboro, Sanford, Carthage, Siler City, and Asheboro, each offer distinct real estate markets shaped by unique trends and demographic influences. This chapter provides an in-depth analysis of these dynamics, offering detailed insights into current trends, future economic prospects, and actionable advice for navigating these diverse markets.

Pittsboro: Sustainability at Its Core

Current Trends: Pittsboro's real estate market is rapidly evolving, driven by a strong demand for sustainable living. This trend is characterized by a growing inventory of eco-friendly homes that appeal to environmentally conscious buyers. The median home price has seen a steady increase, reflecting the area's growing popularity among young professionals and retirees alike.

Demographics: The town's population is on a steady incline, with a significant proportion of residents involved in professions that align with the area's focus on sustainability, such as environmental science and agriculture.

Future Economic Prospects: The Chatham Park development is set to revolutionize Pittsboro, introducing approximately 22,000 new homes and multiple commercial properties. This massive project aims to blend residential, commercial, and recreational spaces with an emphasis on green technology and sustainable practices.

Navigating the Market: For those interested in Pittsboro, properties near the Chatham Park development are particularly promising. Investing in homes with sustainable features or potential for green upgrades is advisable, as the town's ethos strongly supports ecological stewardship.

Sanford: Industrial Past Paving the Way for a Tech-Driven Future

Current Trends: Sanford's market is diversifying, moving away from its industrial roots towards a more technology-focused economy. This shift is reflected in the housing market with an increased demand for modern, urban-style living spaces in the downtown area. The average home price is competitive but rising, influenced by the town's accessibility to major cities and employment hubs.

Demographics: Sanford boasts a diverse population with a mix of blue-collar and white-collar workers. Recent trends show a rise in the number of tech professionals and entrepreneurs in the area.

Future Economic Prospects: The city's strategic plan includes attracting tech startups and enhancing the local infrastructure to support higher-tech industries. This economic shift is expected to bring in a wave of younger, tech-savvy professionals looking for housing.

Navigating the Market: Buyers should focus on newly revitalized neighborhoods where historic properties are being converted into contemporary living spaces. These areas offer both charm and growth potential.

Carthage: Small Town with Big Appeal

Current Trends: Carthage maintains a stable real estate market with consistent demand for single-family homes, which make up the majority of the housing stock. Prices are relatively affordable compared to larger metropolitan areas, making it attractive to first-time homebuyers and retirees.

Demographics: The population in Carthage is older on average than in more urban areas, with a significant percentage of residents aged 55 and over. This demographic trend supports a steady demand for single-level homes and low-maintenance living options.

Future Economic Prospects: Plans to enhance local amenities and community facilities are underway, aiming to increase the town's attractiveness to both older residents and young families.

Navigating the Market: Prospective buyers should look at properties that cater to the needs of the aging population, such as homes without stairs and with accessible facilities. Properties in close proximity to the town center and medical facilities are also wise investments.

Siler City: A Cultural Melting Pot Expanding Rapidly

Current Trends: Siler City is experiencing growth in its real estate market, fueled by its cultural diversity and affordable housing. The town is becoming increasingly popular among artists and creatives, drawn by initiatives like the NC Arts Incubator.

Demographics: The town has a rich mix of cultural backgrounds, with a significant Latino population contributing to the community's vibrant cultural scene.

Future Economic Prospects: Continued investments in arts and cultural sectors are expected to drive property values up, particularly in downtown areas where cultural venues are concentrated.

Navigating the Market: Investing in properties near cultural hotspots or in areas undergoing arts-driven revitalization offers potential for appreciation. Rental properties can also be lucrative, catering to the town's growing population of artists and creatives.

Asheboro: Nature's Haven with Expanding Horizons

Current Trends: Asheboro's real estate market benefits from its scenic beauty and attractions like the North Carolina Zoo. The demand for homes with access to natural settings is high, and property values reflect the town's appeal to tourists and nature lovers.

Demographics: The population is diverse, with a mix of families, young professionals, and retirees. This diversity supports a robust and dynamic real estate market.

Future Economic Prospects: The town is focusing on expanding its tourism sector and leveraging its natural resources to attract more residents and businesses. Developments aimed at enhancing tourist attractions and recreational facilities are expected to spur economic growth and increase property demand.

Navigating the Market: Properties in scenic locales or those offering unique amenities like wildlife access or panoramic views hold particular appeal. The growing tourism sector also presents opportunities for investment in vacation rentals or small businesses that cater to visitors.

Conclusion: Making Informed Choices

Understanding the unique factors at play in the real estate markets of North Carolina's Historic Heartlands is crucial for any potential buyer. Whether you are drawn to the eco-friendly lifestyle of Pittsboro, the burgeoning tech scene in Sanford, the historic charm of Carthage, the cultural richness of Siler City, or the natural beauty of Asheboro, detailed knowledge of these areas will empower you to make informed and successful real estate decisions.

Chapter 3: Moving and Relocation Essentials

Introduction

Relocating to a new home is an exciting journey, but it also requires careful planning and preparation. This chapter will guide you through the essential steps of organizing a successful move to North Carolina's Historic Heartlands, including practical checklists, important contacts, and an overview of local real estate laws and regulations. With these tools, you'll be well-prepared for a smooth transition to Pittsboro, Sanford, Carthage, Siler City, or Asheboro.

Checklist for Planning Your Move

Eight Weeks Before Moving:

1. **Research:** Start by researching your new community. Visit websites, local forums, and social media groups to get a feel for your new home town.

2. **Budget:** Establish a moving budget that includes moving company fees, travel costs, storage, and an emergency fund.

3. **Moving Company:** Obtain quotes from several moving companies. Check reviews and ensure they are licensed and insured.

Six Weeks Before Moving:

1. **Inventory:** Make an inventory of your belongings. Decide what to move, sell, donate, or discard.

2. **Schools:** If you have children, arrange the transfer of school records to their new schools.

3. **Medical Records:** Arrange for the transfer of medical records and prescriptions to new healthcare providers.

Four Weeks Before Moving:

1. **Utilities:** Schedule the disconnection of utilities at your old home and set up utilities at your new home.

2. **Change of Address:** File a change of address with the post office, and notify banks, employers, and insurance providers of your move.

3. **Packing:** Begin packing non-essential items and labeling boxes by room and content.

Two Weeks Before Moving:

1. **Valuables:** Secure important documents and valuables in a safe box that you will personally transport.
2. **Confirmations:** Reconfirm the moving date and details with the moving company.
3. **Essentials Kit:** Pack an essentials kit for moving day that includes toiletries, medications, chargers, snacks, and a few days' worths of clothing.

Moving Day:

1. **Supervision:** Be present to supervise the movers and ensure all items are accounted for during loading.
2. **Final Walkthrough:** Do a final walkthrough of your old home to make sure nothing is left behind.
3. **Essentials:** Ensure that your essentials kit is accessible during the move.

Essential Contacts and Resources for a Smooth Transition

Local Government: Each town has a town hall that can provide information on local services, voting registration, and community events.

Utility Companies: Contact local providers for electricity, water, gas, and internet services to set up new accounts.

Schools: Get in touch with the local school districts to enroll children and learn about the educational system.

Healthcare Providers: Identify local doctors, dentists, and hospitals, and transfer medical records.

Real Estate Assistance: For personalized assistance in buying a home in these towns, contact Crystal Hutchinson, a licensed real estate broker in North Carolina. With extensive knowledge of local markets and a strong commitment to helping families relocate smoothly, Crystal can be reached through her social media on Instagram and TikTok at RealNCLiving_Crystal, on Facebook at Living in NC with Crystal, or via email at crystalsellsnchomes@gmail.com.

Understanding Local Real Estate Laws and Regulations

Local Zoning Laws: Familiarize yourself with the zoning laws in your new town to understand what types of modifications you can make to your property.

Homeowners Associations (HOAs):

- **What are HOAs?** HOAs are organizations in a subdivision, planned community, or condominium that make and enforce rules for the properties and their residents. If you buy a property in a community with an HOA, you automatically become a member and are required to pay dues, known as HOA fees.

- **Impact on Home Buying Decisions:** HOAs can significantly influence your living experience and financial obligations. They may have rules that impact home color, landscaping, renovations, and parking. Fees can vary widely and might cover amenities such as pools, fitness centers, and security. Violating HOA rules can result in fines and other penalties.

Local Real Estate Taxes: Understand the property tax rates in your area, as they can vary significantly and impact your budget.

Conclusion

Moving to a new home is a significant life event that, with the right preparation, can be an enjoyable and exciting transition. By following these checklists and utilizing the provided contacts and resources, you'll be better prepared to navigate the complexities of relocating. Always remember that understanding local real estate laws, including HOA regulations, is crucial in making informed decisions that align with your lifestyle and financial goals.

Chapter 4: Community and Social Life

Introduction

The essence of a place is not just defined by its geography and architecture but also by the vibrancy of its community and the richness of its social life. In North Carolina's Historic Heartlands, each town—Pittsboro, Sanford, Carthage, Siler City, and Asheboro—offers a unique tapestry of community groups, social opportunities, and annual events that cater to families, retirees, and young professionals alike. This chapter explores the dynamic social scenes of these towns, highlighting how new residents can integrate and find their niche.

Pittsboro: A Hub of Artistic and Environmental Communities

Community Organizations: Pittsboro is known for its environmental initiatives and artistic communities. Organizations like the Chatham Arts Council and the Pittsboro Environmental Group foster engagement through educational programs and community projects. These groups offer opportunities for residents to contribute to sustainable practices and engage in local arts.

Social Opportunities: The town's vibrant farmer's market and various eco-friendly events provide a social calendar filled with activities that appeal to families and environmental enthusiasts. The annual Pittsboro Street Fair, which showcases local crafts, food, and entertainment, is a must-attend for community bonding.

Annual Festivities: Pittsboro celebrates its unique blend of arts and sustainable living with events like the Pittsboro First Sunday Artisan Fair and the Chatham County Fair, which bring together the best of local crafts, music, and agricultural products.

Sanford: A Blend of Cultural Diversity and Industrial Heritage

Community Organizations: Sanford's rich history in pottery and brick manufacturing is preserved by groups such as the Sanford Historical Society and the Lee County Community Orchestra. These organizations offer educational workshops and cultural events that celebrate Sanford's heritage and diversity.

Social Opportunities: For young professionals and families, Sanford provides a mix of cultural and recreational activities.

The vibrant downtown area hosts live music nights and food truck rodeos, offering a perfect setting for socializing and networking.

Annual Festivities: The Sanford Arts & Vine Festival and the Pottery Festival are highlights of the year, drawing artists and visitors from across the state. These events not only celebrate the local arts and crafts but also serve as great social gatherings.

Carthage: Celebrating History with Community Pride

Community Organizations: Carthage is known for its dedication to community service, with numerous volunteer organizations such as the Carthage Book Club and the Carthage Historical Museum. These groups play a crucial role in preserving the town's history and fostering a sense of community among residents.

Social Opportunities: Carthage offers a quiet, family-friendly atmosphere with plenty of opportunities for outdoor enthusiasts and history buffs. The town's community center regularly hosts gatherings, workshops, and classes that cater to all age groups.

Annual Festivities: The Carthage Buggy Festival is a celebrated annual event that honors the town's past as a center for buggy manufacturing. Featuring parades, crafts, and classic car shows, it's a fantastic opportunity for residents to connect and celebrate their heritage.

Siler City: A Cultural Mosaic of Social Engagement

Community Organizations: With a significant focus on cultural diversity, Siler City's community organizations like the Hispanic Liaison and the Siler City Development Organization promote inclusivity and support for all residents. These groups facilitate cultural exchanges and support economic development within the community.

Social Opportunities: Siler City's vibrant art scene is a draw for creatives and young professionals. The NC Arts Incubator, with its galleries and studios, offers classes and events that encourage social interaction and artistic collaboration.

Annual Festivities: The Siler City Latino Festival and the Third Friday Art Walk are key social events that celebrate the town's diverse community. These festivals offer a colorful display of music, dance, and art that brings together families, artists, and community members in a lively celebration.

Asheboro: Nature and Community Converge

Community Organizations: Asheboro's community life is enriched by organizations such as the Asheboro/Randolph Chamber of Commerce and the Asheboro Cultural & Recreation Services. These groups facilitate events and activities that promote community wellness and engagement.

Social Opportunities: For families and nature lovers, Asheboro provides ample opportunities to engage in outdoor activities such as hiking, bird watching, and zoo visits. The town also hosts several sports leagues and outdoor concerts that are perfect for young professionals and families looking to meet new people.

Annual Festivities: The Fall Festival, a two-day event packed with crafts, food, and entertainment, epitomizes Asheboro's community spirit. Additionally, the Zoo City Sports Car Club's Annual Car Show combines a love for classic cars with community fundraising.

Conclusion

The social fabric of Pittsboro, Sanford, Carthage, Siler City, and Asheboro is woven with the threads of vibrant community groups, diverse social opportunities, and enriching annual festivities. Each town offers its unique flavor of community life, catering to a wide range of interests and demographics. Engaging with these communities provides more than just entertainment—it fosters a sense of belonging and shared identity that makes living in North Carolina's Historic Heartlands truly fulfilling.

Chapter 5: Government and Public Services

Introduction

Effective government and robust public services are the backbone of any thriving community. In North Carolina's Historic Heartlands, the towns of Pittsboro, Sanford, Carthage, Siler City, and Asheboro each offer well-organized government structures and comprehensive public services that cater to the needs of their residents. This chapter delves into the local government setups, the essential services provided, and the public transportation systems of these towns, providing new residents with vital information for navigating their new community environments efficiently.

Pittsboro: Progressive Governance and Community-Focused Services

Local Government: Pittsboro operates under a council-manager form of government. The town council, elected by the residents, sets policies and strategic directions, while the town manager handles the day-to-day administration, ensuring that the council's decisions are implemented effectively.

Essential Services:

- **Healthcare:** Pittsboro is served by several clinics and specialty medical services, with larger hospital facilities accessible in nearby Chapel Hill and Durham.

- **Emergency Services:** The town maintains a well-equipped fire department and a responsive police force. Emergency medical services are coordinated through Chatham County.

Public Transportation: Public transportation in Pittsboro includes county-operated transit services that offer both fixed-route and demand-response services, making local travel and connections to neighboring areas convenient for residents without personal vehicles.

Sanford: Industrial Heritage with Modern Public Infrastructure

Local Government: Sanford utilizes a mayor-council form of government. The mayor and the city council work together to legislate and guide the city's growth, focusing on maintaining a balance between preserving its industrial heritage and fostering new economic opportunities.

Essential Services:

- **Healthcare:** Sanford residents have access to Central Carolina Hospital, along with a variety of private practices and specialty medical providers.

- **Emergency Services:** The city is well-covered by its own police and fire departments, providing swift response times and community safety programs.

Public Transportation: Sanford's public transportation includes the Lee County Transit System, which offers routes covering the city and connections to broader regional services. This service is essential for facilitating access to jobs, healthcare, and education.

Carthage: Small-Town Feel with Efficient Local Management

Local Government: Carthage is governed by a mayor and a board of commissioners who are deeply involved in the community. This governance structure allows for high responsiveness to local needs, with an emphasis on maintaining the town's historic character and community values.

Essential Services:

- **Healthcare:** While smaller than its larger neighbors, Carthage provides adequate healthcare facilities for routine medical needs and has arrangements with nearby larger hospitals for more specialized care.

- **Emergency Services:** Carthage prides itself on a volunteer fire department and a local police department that emphasize community interaction and safety.

Public Transportation:

The transportation services in Carthage are limited but growing, with community shuttles and regional connections that support the town's less mobile residents and those commuting to jobs outside the town.

Siler City: Embracing Diversity with Effective Public Services

Local Government: Siler City operates under a town council form of government where council members represent various districts within the town, ensuring diverse community representation. The mayor plays a more ceremonial role, with the town manager overseeing daily operations.

Essential Services:

- **Healthcare:** Siler City has several healthcare centers, including a community health center that caters to the underserved populations, ensuring that all residents have access to necessary medical care.

- **Emergency Services:** Comprehensive emergency services are provided by dedicated police and fire departments, with enhanced focus on bilingual services to cater to the town's diverse population.

Public Transportation: Siler City's public transportation system is designed to serve a wide array of needs, focusing on inclusivity with services that accommodate the town's diverse and multilingual populace.

Asheboro: Nature-Centric Governance with Comprehensive Services

Local Government: Asheboro uses a council-manager system, where the city council includes members elected at-large and the city manager administers the implementation of their policies. This structure supports clear and effective governance, aligning with the city's focus on community welfare and environmental conservation.

Essential Services:

- **Healthcare:** Asheboro is well equipped with a regional hospital and numerous clinics, providing comprehensive healthcare services.

- **Emergency Services:** The city's emergency services are robust, with a particular emphasis on quick response capabilities and community disaster preparedness.

Public Transportation: Asheboro offers regional bus services that connect residents to major areas within and outside the city, facilitating easy access to urban centers.

Conclusion

The governance structures and public services across Pittsboro, Sanford, Carthage, Siler City, and Asheboro demonstrate their commitment to maintaining high-quality living standards for their residents. From responsive local governments to comprehensive healthcare and transportation options, these towns ensure that their communities remain vibrant and well-serviced, fostering environments where residents can thrive.

Chapter 6: Education and Local Schools

Introduction

Education is a cornerstone of community life and personal development. In the towns of Pittsboro, Sanford, Carthage, Siler City, and Asheboro in North Carolina's Historic Heartlands, the dedication to providing top-quality education is evident in the variety and depth of the educational institutions available. This chapter offers a comprehensive guide to the schools in each town, covering public, private, and special programs, along with extracurricular activities and resources for evaluating school performance and community feedback.

Pittsboro: A Community Committed to Diverse Educational Pathways

Educational Institutions: Pittsboro's educational landscape is rich and varied, featuring schools that cater to a range of educational needs and interests:

- **Public Schools:** Chatham County Schools serve Pittsboro with several noteworthy institutions. Pittsboro

Elementary and Horton Middle School are known for their strong community involvement and innovative teaching methods. Northwood High School is recognized for its advanced academic programs and strong sports teams.

- **Charter Schools:** Woods Charter School offers a unique educational approach, focusing on student-led learning and environmental sustainability, making it a popular choice among families.

- **Private Schools:** Thales Academy Pittsboro provides a rigorous classical education that emphasizes character development and academic excellence from kindergarten through high school.

Special Programs and Extracurricular Activities: Pittsboro schools offer a range of special programs that enhance the educational experience:

- **Environmental Programs:** Many schools incorporate environmental education, teaching students the importance of sustainability and conservation.

- **Arts and Music:** Northwood High School's arts programs are particularly strong, with opportunities in theater, music, and fine arts that encourage students to engage creatively.

Resources for School Ratings and Feedback: Parents can access detailed school performance reports through the North Carolina Department of Public Instruction's website. Local community forums and websites like GreatSchools.org also offer user-generated reviews and ratings.

Sanford: Fostering Growth Through Education

Educational Institutions: Sanford's robust school system is designed to support a growing community with diverse educational needs:

- **Public Schools:** Lee County Schools operates several elementary schools such as B.T. Bullock Elementary, which has a strong focus on technology integration in the classroom. SanLee Middle School and Lee County High School offer comprehensive academic and extracurricular programs that cater to a diverse student body.

- **Specialty Schools:** Lee Early College provides an opportunity for students to earn an associate degree alongside their high school diploma, catering especially to those looking to advance quickly in their academic or career paths.

- **Private Schools:** Grace Christian School offers an alternative religious-based education for families seeking a Christian educational environment with rigorous academic standards.

Special Programs and Extracurricular Activities:

- **STEM Focus:** Many schools in Sanford, including Lee County High School, emphasize STEM education, preparing students for careers in science, technology, engineering, and math through specialized courses and hands-on learning experiences.

- **Sports and Clubs:** Sanford schools boast a wide range of sports teams and clubs, from traditional athletics to special interest groups like robotics and debate, fostering a well-rounded educational experience.

Resources for School Ratings and Feedback: The North Carolina School Report Cards provide detailed insights into the academic and extracurricular standards of schools in Sanford. Additionally, platforms like Niche.com offer reviews from students and parents that give a personal perspective on the school environments.

Carthage: Emphasizing Tradition and Innovation in Education

Educational Institutions: Carthage's educational offerings reflect its commitment to both tradition and modern educational trends:

- **Public Schools:** Part of Moore County Schools, Carthage features institutions like Carthage Elementary, which is celebrated for its community-centric approach, and New Century Middle School, known for its innovative teaching methods. Union Pines High School is renowned for its high academic standards and strong athletic programs.

- **Private Education:** The O'Neal School provides an independent, college-preparatory education from pre-K through twelfth grade, offering a personalized approach to student development.

Special Programs and Extracurricular Activities:

- **Vocational Training:** Union Pines High School offers vocational programs in fields such as automotive technology and carpentry, which are designed to provide students with practical skills that can lead directly to employment or further education in technical fields.

- **Extracurricular Activities:** Beyond academics, schools in Carthage offer a variety of clubs and activities that cater to diverse interests, including environmental clubs, arts programs, and leadership training opportunities.

Resources for School Ratings and Feedback: Moore County Schools' website provides comprehensive performance data, and other resources like SchoolDigger.com help parents evaluate schools based on a variety of criteria, including student achievement and extracurricular offerings.

Siler City: A Rich Tapestry of Cultural and Educational Opportunities

Educational Institutions: Siler City's commitment to educational excellence is evident in its range of schools and programs:

- **Public Schools:** Jordan-Matthews High School stands out for its strong academic programs and commitment to cultural inclusivity. Chatham Middle School offers a robust curriculum tailored to meet the needs of its diverse student population.

- **Charter and Private Schools:** Chatham Charter School in nearby Siler City offers a K-12 education that fosters academic excellence and civic responsibility. Additionally, private options like St. Julia Catholic School provide alternatives that focus on moral development along with academic rigor.

Special Programs and Extracurricular Activities:

- **Language and Cultural Programs:** Given its diverse population, Siler City schools offer extensive ESL programs and cultural integration initiatives that help students from various backgrounds thrive together.

- **Arts and Athletics:** Jordan-Matthews High School is particularly noted for its strong arts programs, including band, drama, and visual arts, which are complemented by an array of sports and other extracurricular activities.

Resources for School Ratings and Feedback: Resources like the U.S. Department of Education's National Center for Education Statistics provide detailed data on schools in Siler City, while local community feedback can be accessed through platforms like Facebook groups and local education forums.

Asheboro: Comprehensive Education in a Supportive Community

Educational Institutions: Asheboro offers a wide spectrum of educational institutions designed to cater to the holistic development of its students:

- **Public Schools:** Asheboro City Schools, including Asheboro High School, are known for their comprehensive educational programs and strong community support. South Asheboro Middle School and Charles W McCrary Elementary are notable for their innovative programs and dedicated faculty.

- **Specialty Programs:** Asheboro High's Zoo School program is a standout, offering unique educational experiences in partnership with the North Carolina Zoo.

Special Programs and Extracurricular Activities:

- **Specialized Academics:** The Zoo School program at Asheboro High School allows students to engage in real-world conservation projects, providing invaluable hands-on learning experiences.

- **Extracurricular Diversity:** Asheboro schools offer a wide array of extracurricular activities ranging from sports to music and arts, ensuring that all students have the opportunity to explore their interests and talents.

Resources for School Ratings and Feedback: Asheboro City Schools' own websites provide detailed information about each school's offerings, while external resources like GreatSchools.org give insights into school performance based on comprehensive data analysis and parental feedback.

Chapter 7: Healthcare and Emergency Services

Introduction

Access to high-quality healthcare and dependable emergency services is a cornerstone of community well-being, particularly in regions like North Carolina's Historic Heartlands. The towns of Pittsboro, Sanford, Carthage, Siler City, and Asheboro each offer a comprehensive framework of medical and emergency services tailored to meet the diverse needs of their residents. This chapter provides an expanded look at the healthcare facilities, emergency response systems, and wellness initiatives that underscore the commitment of these towns to safeguard and enhance the health of their communities.

Pittsboro: Embracing Holistic Health Practices

Healthcare Facilities: Pittsboro's healthcare infrastructure is both comprehensive and integrative, reflecting its commitment to blending traditional medical treatments with holistic health practices. The cornerstone of healthcare in Pittsboro is Chatham Hospital, part of the UNC Health Care system. This hospital provides essential services, including emergency care, surgical services, and specialized outpatient care. Chatham Hospital is known for its patient-centered approach, emphasizing both quality care and compassionate service.

In addition to traditional healthcare services, Pittsboro is home to several holistic health centers that offer treatments such as acupuncture, massage therapy, and integrative medicine. These centers cater to a growing population interested in sustainable and preventive health approaches. For example, the Pittsboro Center for Natural Medicine offers a wide range of alternative treatments and educational programs focused on wellness and holistic health.

Emergency Services: The emergency services in Pittsboro are well-coordinated and highly responsive, ensuring the safety and well-being of all residents. The town's emergency response infrastructure includes a dedicated volunteer fire department known for its efficiency and community engagement. The Pittsboro Police Department prioritizes community policing, working closely with residents to maintain public safety and address local concerns. Emergency medical services (EMS) in Pittsboro are integrated with county services, ensuring quick response times and comprehensive coverage across both urban and rural areas.

Wellness and Preventive Health Programs: Pittsboro is proactive in promoting health and wellness through a variety of community initiatives. Regular health fairs provide residents with access to screenings, flu shots, and educational workshops on topics ranging from mental health to chronic disease management. The town also encourages outdoor activities with well-maintained parks and trails, which support physical health and community engagement. Local yoga studios often offer classes in parks to increase public access to stress reduction and physical fitness programs.

Sanford: A Hub of Comprehensive Medical Services

Healthcare Facilities: Sanford's healthcare infrastructure is robust, centered around Central Carolina Hospital, a full-service medical facility that provides a comprehensive range of medical services. Central Carolina Hospital features a state-of-the-art emergency room, a heart center offering advanced cardiac care, and maternity services that include prenatal and postnatal care. The hospital is supported by an array of specialty clinics and private practices that address a broad spectrum of healthcare needs, ensuring that residents have access to both primary and specialized medical care.

Sanford also hosts numerous specialty clinics that cater to various health needs, including pediatric health, women's health, and geriatric care. These clinics provide essential services such as routine check-ups, vaccinations, and chronic disease management, contributing to the overall health of the community.

Emergency Services: Sanford's emergency services are comprehensive and well-integrated. The city maintains a professional fire department equipped with the latest firefighting technology and trained personnel capable of handling a wide range of emergencies. The police force is similarly advanced, utilizing modern emergency response techniques and community policing strategies to ensure public safety. The Lee County EMS is renowned for its rapid response and high-quality medical care, employing advanced life support techniques and continuous staff training to maintain high standards of emergency care.

Wellness and Preventive Health Programs: Sanford places a strong emphasis on preventive health and wellness, offering a variety of community health programs designed to promote active living and disease prevention. The Sanford Parks and Recreation Department organizes numerous fitness classes, sports leagues, and outdoor activities that encourage physical activity among residents of all ages. Additionally, the city hosts health education seminars on topics such as diabetes management, smoking cessation, and mental health, aimed at providing residents with the knowledge and resources to maintain a healthy lifestyle.

Carthage: Focused on Family and Senior Health Services

Healthcare Facilities: Carthage offers excellent healthcare services through facilities like FirstHealth Moore Regional Hospital - Carthage, which provides a wide range of medical services including emergency care, comprehensive diagnostic facilities, and specialized treatment options. The hospital is particularly known for its geriatric care, offering services tailored to the needs of older adults, such as memory care and rehabilitation programs.

Local clinics in Carthage complement the hospital's services by providing accessible healthcare options for families and individuals. These clinics focus on preventive care, routine check-ups, and chronic disease management, ensuring that residents receive comprehensive healthcare close to home.

Emergency Services: Carthage's emergency services are designed to meet the needs of a smaller community, with a strong emphasis on accessibility and community relations. The town's volunteer fire department is highly regarded for its quick response times and effective firefighting capabilities. The Carthage Police Department maintains a proactive approach to public safety, emphasizing community engagement and preventive measures to reduce crime and enhance public trust. The local EMS is known for its efficiency and compassionate care, particularly in managing emergencies involving older adults and individuals with chronic health conditions.

Wellness and Preventive Health Programs: Carthage places a significant focus on wellness and preventive health, particularly for its aging population. The town offers numerous programs aimed at promoting health and well-being among seniors, including fitness classes tailored to older adults, health education sessions on topics such as arthritis management and diabetes prevention, and community activities that encourage social interaction and physical activity. These programs are often held at local community centers and senior centers, providing convenient access for residents.

Siler City: Addressing Health Needs in a Diverse Community

Healthcare Facilities: Siler City's healthcare infrastructure is designed to meet the needs of its diverse population, with facilities that provide comprehensive and culturally competent care. The Chatham Hospital branch in Siler City offers emergency services, general healthcare, and specialized care for a diverse population, including significant Latino and migrant communities. The hospital is supported by several community clinics that focus on providing bilingual health services and culturally appropriate care.

These clinics offer a range of services, including family medicine, pediatric care, and women's health services, ensuring that all community members have access to quality healthcare. The inclusion of language translation services and community health workers who understand the cultural needs of the population enhances the effectiveness of these services.

Emergency Services: Siler City's emergency services are known for their inclusivity and effectiveness. The town maintains a comprehensive setup of police, fire, and EMS services that are equipped to handle a variety of emergencies. The fire department, police, and EMS work closely with community leaders and organizations to ensure that all residents, regardless of language or background, receive prompt and effective emergency responses.

The fire department conducts regular safety drills and fire prevention workshops in schools and community centers, while the police department engages in community policing initiatives to build trust and ensure public safety. The EMS provides swift medical responses, with personnel trained to address the specific needs of a culturally diverse population.

Wellness and Preventive Health Programs: Siler City champions wellness through a variety of community health initiatives designed to engage various cultural groups. These programs include bilingual health education sessions, community fitness classes, and health fairs that offer screenings and educational materials in multiple languages. The town also hosts cultural festivals and events that promote health and wellness, providing opportunities for residents to learn about healthy living in a fun and engaging environment.

Asheboro: Comprehensive Healthcare in a Growing City

Healthcare Facilities: Asheboro's healthcare system is anchored by Randolph Health, which offers a broad range of medical services including an emergency department, specialized women's health services, and extensive inpatient and outpatient facilities. Randolph Health is known for its high standards of care and patient-centered approach, providing services such as surgical care, cancer treatment, and rehabilitation programs.

In addition to Randolph Health, Asheboro is home to numerous private practices and specialty clinics that enhance the healthcare landscape. These facilities offer services such as primary care, dental care, mental health counseling, and physical therapy, ensuring that residents have access to comprehensive and specialized care.

Emergency Services: Asheboro boasts an integrated emergency services system that includes a professional firefighting unit, a dedicated police force, and an EMS renowned for its effectiveness. The fire department is equipped with advanced firefighting technology and conducts regular training exercises to maintain high standards of readiness. The police department focuses on community policing and crime prevention, working closely with residents to ensure public safety.

The EMS provides swift and efficient medical responses, with personnel trained in advanced life support and emergency care techniques. These services collaborate to offer comprehensive emergency preparedness and response programs, including community CPR training, emergency readiness workshops, and public safety campaigns.

Wellness and Preventive Health Programs: Asheboro promotes a holistic approach to health with numerous wellness programs that address physical, mental, and emotional well-being. The city offers community-wide fitness challenges, health education programs in schools and community centers, and preventive screenings provided through local healthcare facilities. The Randolph Health Wellness Center provides resources for exercise and nutrition, including fitness classes, personal training, and wellness workshops.

The city also supports mental health initiatives, offering counseling services and support groups for residents dealing with issues such as depression, anxiety, and substance abuse. These programs aim to reduce stigma and provide accessible mental health care for all community members.

Conclusion

In the Historic Heartlands of North Carolina, the towns of Pittsboro, Sanford, Carthage, Siler City, and Asheboro each demonstrate a strong commitment to healthcare and emergency services, tailored to meet the needs of their diverse populations. With a focus on comprehensive care, rapid emergency response, and proactive wellness programs, these communities ensure that their residents have access to essential services that promote and maintain health and safety. This commitment not only enhances the quality of life for current residents but also makes these towns attractive to potential newcomers looking for a supportive and caring community environment.

Chapter 8: Parks, Recreation, and Green Living

Introduction

The heartbeat of any vibrant community often lies in its parks, recreational spaces, and green living initiatives. These elements foster social connections, promote health and wellness, and underscore a community's commitment to sustainability. North Carolina's Historic Heartlands—Pittsboro, Sanford, Carthage, Siler City, and Asheboro—are no exception. Each town offers unique opportunities for outdoor activities, family outings, and sustainable living. This chapter explores the major parks, recreational areas, and green initiatives that make these towns not just places to live, but places to thrive.

Pittsboro: A Sanctuary for Nature Lovers

Major Parks and Recreational Areas: Pittsboro boasts a variety of parks and green spaces that cater to nature enthusiasts and families alike.

The **Jordan Lake State Recreation Area** is a crown jewel, offering over 1,000 acres of water and surrounding woodlands. It's perfect for boating, fishing, hiking, and camping.

Rock Ridge Park, with its extensive trails, disc golf course, and playgrounds, is another popular spot for both relaxation and adventure.

Opportunities for Outdoor Activities and Family Outings: The abundance of outdoor activities in Pittsboro ensures that there is something for everyone. Families can enjoy picnicking by the lake, kayaking, or participating in guided nature tours at Jordan Lake. Rock Ridge Park offers family-friendly hiking trails, picnic shelters, and open spaces for recreational sports.

The **Haw River** also provides opportunities for kayaking and canoeing, allowing residents to immerse themselves in the natural beauty of the area.

Initiatives in Sustainability and Green Living: Pittsboro is committed to sustainability, with numerous initiatives aimed at promoting green living. The town supports local agriculture through its vibrant farmers' markets and community-supported agriculture (CSA) programs.

Pittsboro's **Abundance Foundation** promotes sustainable living through educational workshops on renewable energy, organic farming, and eco-friendly construction. The town also encourages the use of renewable energy, with several solar farms and incentives for homeowners to install solar panels.

Sanford: A Hub of Recreational Diversity

Major Parks and Recreational Areas: Sanford's parks and recreation system is extensive, featuring a blend of urban parks, sports complexes, and natural preserves.

San-Lee Park is a standout, with over 177 acres of trails, lakes, and educational centers.

Depot Park in downtown Sanford is a community gathering spot, hosting concerts, farmers' markets, and festivals.

The **Endor Iron Furnace** offers a historical site combined with nature trails, adding a unique twist to outdoor recreation.

Opportunities for Outdoor Activities and Family Outings: San-Lee Park is a haven for outdoor enthusiasts, offering hiking and mountain biking trails, paddle boating, and fishing. The park's nature center provides educational programs and exhibits on local wildlife and ecology, making it an excellent destination for family outings. Depot Park's open spaces and playgrounds are perfect for children, while its event calendar keeps the community engaged year-round. The Endor Iron Furnace, with its historical significance and surrounding trails, provides a unique blend of education and outdoor activity.

Initiatives in Sustainability and Green Living: Sanford is active in promoting sustainability through various community programs and initiatives. The city has invested in green infrastructure, such as rain gardens and permeable pavements, to manage stormwater and reduce runoff. Sanford's **Tree City USA** designation reflects its commitment to urban forestry and green space preservation. Additionally, the city supports recycling programs and hosts environmental education events to raise awareness about sustainable living practices.

Carthage: Preserving Green Spaces with a Historic Touch

Major Parks and Recreational Areas: Carthage offers a mix of historical sites and natural parks that appeal to residents of all ages.

Hillcrest Park is a popular destination with its sports fields, playgrounds, and walking trails.

Nick's Creek Preserve provides a tranquil escape with its scenic trails and opportunities for bird watching. The town also features smaller community parks that offer open spaces for recreation and relaxation.

Opportunities for Outdoor Activities and Family Outings: Hillcrest Park is the hub of recreational activity in Carthage, offering facilities for soccer, baseball, and tennis, as well as playgrounds and picnic areas. Nick's Creek Preserve is ideal for nature walks, hiking, and observing wildlife, providing a peaceful retreat for families and nature lovers. The town's smaller parks offer spaces for community events, family gatherings, and casual sports activities.

Initiatives in Sustainability and Green Living: Carthage is dedicated to preserving its natural beauty and promoting sustainability. The town participates in the **North Carolina GreenTravel Initiative**, which encourages sustainable tourism practices. Local schools and community groups often engage in environmental projects, such as tree planting and clean-up drives. Carthage also supports local farmers through its farmers' market, promoting organic produce and sustainable agriculture.

Siler City: A Blend of Culture and Nature

Major Parks and Recreational Areas: Siler City is home to several parks that cater to diverse recreational needs.

Bray Park is a central hub, offering sports facilities, playgrounds, and a community center.

Boling Lane Park provides a more natural setting with walking trails and picnic areas. The town's parks are designed to support both active recreation and tranquil escapes.

Opportunities for Outdoor Activities and Family Outings: Bray Park's sports facilities, including basketball courts, soccer fields, and a swimming pool, make it a popular spot for families and sports enthusiasts. The park also hosts community events and recreational programs throughout the year. Boling Lane Park offers a peaceful environment for walking, picnicking, and enjoying nature. The town's parks and recreation department organizes various activities, such as youth sports leagues, fitness classes, and cultural festivals, ensuring there is always something happening for residents to enjoy.

Initiatives in Sustainability and Green Living: Siler City actively promotes sustainability through community initiatives and educational programs. The town's **Green Growth Toolbox** program helps integrate conservation practices into local planning and development. Siler City also participates in energy efficiency programs, encouraging residents and businesses to adopt renewable energy solutions. The town's farmers' market supports local agriculture and provides access to fresh, sustainably grown produce.

Asheboro: Nature and Community at its Core

Major Parks and Recreational Areas: Asheboro offers an extensive network of parks and recreational facilities that highlight the town's natural beauty and commitment to community well-being.

The **North Carolina Zoo** is a major attraction, featuring expansive natural habitats and diverse wildlife.

Bicentennial Park in downtown Asheboro hosts concerts, festivals, and farmers' markets, making it a lively community gathering spot.

Lake Lucas and **Lake Reese** provide opportunities for boating, fishing, and picnicking, while

Richland Creek Canopy Tours offers thrilling zip-line adventures.

Opportunities for Outdoor Activities and Family Outings: The North Carolina Zoo is a must-visit for families, offering educational programs, animal encounters, and expansive trails. Bicentennial Park's events and open spaces make it perfect for family outings and community gatherings. Lake Lucas and Lake

Reese are popular for water-based activities such as kayaking, paddleboarding, and fishing. Richland Creek Canopy Tours provides an exciting outdoor adventure with zip-lining and eco-tours, attracting both residents and tourists.

Initiatives in Sustainability and Green Living: Asheboro is a leader in sustainability, with initiatives aimed at preserving natural resources and promoting green living. The North Carolina Zoo plays a significant role in conservation efforts, focusing on wildlife preservation and environmental education. Asheboro's **Sustainable Asheboro** program promotes recycling, energy efficiency, and sustainable development practices. The city also supports community gardens and local food initiatives, encouraging residents to engage in sustainable agriculture and healthy eating.

Conclusion

The parks, recreational areas, and green living initiatives in Pittsboro, Sanford, Carthage, Siler City, and Asheboro highlight the vibrant community spirit and commitment to sustainability that characterize North Carolina's Historic Heartlands. Each town offers unique opportunities for outdoor activities, family outings, and environmental stewardship, making these communities not just places to live, but places to thrive.

Whether it's enjoying a hike in a local park, participating in a community event, or engaging in sustainable practices, residents of these towns have ample opportunities to connect with nature and each other, fostering a strong sense of community and well-being.

Chapter 9: Economic Opportunities and Employment

Introduction

Economic vitality and employment opportunities are crucial components of a thriving community. In North Carolina's Historic Heartlands, the towns of Pittsboro, Sanford, Carthage, Siler City, and Asheboro each have unique economic landscapes shaped by major employers, emerging industries, and evolving job markets. This chapter provides an in-depth look at the economic opportunities and employment trends in these towns, highlighting the significant impact of the tech and healthcare sectors on their local economies.

Pittsboro: A Growing Hub for Sustainable Business

Major Employers: Pittsboro's economy is diverse, with a strong emphasis on sustainability and small business development. Major employers in the area include:

- **Chatham Park:** A large-scale, mixed-use development that is becoming a significant employment hub with opportunities in construction, retail, healthcare, and technology.

- **Piedmont Health Services:** Providing essential healthcare services and employment opportunities in the region.

- **Small and Local Businesses:** The vibrant downtown area hosts numerous small businesses, including restaurants, shops, and professional services.

Employment Trends and Job Opportunities: Pittsboro is experiencing growth in sustainable and green industries. There is a rising demand for jobs in renewable energy, organic farming, and eco-friendly construction. The proximity to Research Triangle Park (RTP) also creates opportunities for remote work and tech-related positions.

Impact of Tech and Healthcare Sectors: The tech sector's influence is growing, particularly with initiatives at Chatham Park attracting tech startups and innovation-driven companies. Healthcare remains a robust sector, with Piedmont Health Services and other local clinics expanding their services, creating more healthcare jobs.

Sanford: Diversified Economic Base with Growing Tech Influence

Major Employers: Sanford's economy is well-rounded, with significant contributions from manufacturing, healthcare, and education. Major employers include:

- **Pfizer:** A leading pharmaceutical company with a substantial manufacturing presence in Sanford.

- **Central Carolina Hospital:** Providing a wide range of healthcare services and employment.

- **Coty Inc.:** A global beauty company with manufacturing facilities in Sanford.

- **Sanford Contractors:** One of the largest contractors in the region, contributing to the local economy through various construction projects.

Employment Trends and Job Opportunities: Sanford is seeing a resurgence in manufacturing jobs, with companies like Pfizer and Coty expanding their operations. The construction industry is also growing, driven by infrastructure projects and residential development. Additionally, there is an increasing number of job opportunities in the tech sector, spurred by initiatives to attract tech companies to the area.

Impact of Tech and Healthcare Sectors: The tech sector's growth is enhancing job diversity in Sanford, with a focus on tech-driven manufacturing and biotech industries. Healthcare continues to be a major employer, with Central Carolina Hospital expanding its services to meet the growing population's needs.

Carthage: Balancing Tradition with Modern Growth

Major Employers: Carthage has a balanced economy with significant contributions from healthcare, education, and local government. Major employers include:

- **FirstHealth Moore Regional Hospital - Carthage:** A major healthcare provider and employer in the region.
- **Moore County Schools:** Providing educational services and employment for educators and support staff.
- **County Government:** Offering a range of jobs in public administration and community services.

Employment Trends and Job Opportunities: Carthage is experiencing steady growth in the healthcare sector, driven by the needs of its aging population. Education and local government remain stable sources of employment. There is also a growing interest in tourism and hospitality, leveraging the town's historical charm.

Impact of Tech and Healthcare Sectors: Healthcare is the dominant sector, with FirstHealth Moore Regional Hospital - Carthage expanding its services and workforce. While tech has a smaller footprint in Carthage, there are emerging opportunities in telehealth and tech-driven educational tools.

Siler City: Embracing Diversity and Industrial Growth

Major Employers: Siler City's economy is diverse, with strong industrial and agricultural sectors. Major employers include:

- **Mountaire Farms:** A major poultry processing company providing numerous jobs in the region.
- **Chatham Hospital:** A key healthcare provider and employer in Siler City.
- **Engineered Plastic Components (EPC):** A manufacturing company contributing significantly to local employment.

Employment Trends and Job Opportunities: Siler City is seeing growth in manufacturing and agriculture, with companies like Mountaire Farms and EPC expanding their operations. There is also a notable increase in healthcare jobs, driven by the needs of a growing population and the expansion of Chatham Hospital.

Impact of Tech and Healthcare Sectors: While the tech sector is not as prominent, there is potential growth in tech-related manufacturing. Healthcare continues to expand, with Chatham Hospital adding more specialized services and increasing its workforce to meet community needs.

Asheboro: A Blend of Industry and Innovation

Major Employers: Asheboro's economy is robust, with significant contributions from manufacturing, healthcare, and retail. Major employers include:

- **Randolph Health:** The primary healthcare provider in Asheboro.
- **Technimark:** A global plastics manufacturer with facilities in Asheboro.

- **Klaussner Home Furnishings:** A leading furniture manufacturer and employer in the region.

Employment Trends and Job Opportunities: Asheboro is experiencing growth in advanced manufacturing, healthcare, and retail. Technimark and Klaussner Home Furnishings are expanding their operations, creating more manufacturing jobs. The healthcare sector is also growing, with Randolph Health enhancing its services and facilities.

Impact of Tech and Healthcare Sectors: The tech sector is influencing manufacturing processes, with companies like Technimark adopting advanced technologies to improve efficiency and product quality. Healthcare remains a significant employer, with Randolph Health expanding its services to accommodate a growing and aging population.

Conclusion

The towns of Pittsboro, Sanford, Carthage, Siler City, and Asheboro each present unique economic opportunities and employment landscapes. With major employers spanning healthcare, manufacturing, education, and tech sectors, these towns are poised for growth and innovation. The influence of tech and healthcare sectors is particularly notable, driving job creation and economic development. For residents and newcomers alike, these towns offer a dynamic environment for employment and career growth, underpinned by a strong sense of community and forward-thinking economic strategies.

Chapter 10: Homebuying and Financial Planning

Introduction

Buying a home is a significant milestone, often accompanied by excitement and anxiety. The process can be complex, especially in a competitive market. This chapter aims to demystify the homebuying journey by providing practical advice on dealing with bidding wars, essential financial planning tips for first-time homebuyers, and an overview of mortgage basics and helpful planning tools.

Dealing with Bidding Wars and Housing Demand

In competitive real estate markets, bidding wars can be common, driven by high demand and limited supply. Here are some strategies to navigate these challenging situations:

1. Get Pre-Approved for a Mortgage: Before you start house hunting, get pre-approved for a mortgage. A pre-approval letter shows sellers that you are a serious and qualified buyer, which can give you an edge in a bidding war.

2. Know Your Budget: Determine your budget and stick to it. It's easy to get caught up in the excitement of a bidding war, but overextending yourself financially can lead to long-term stress. Work with your real estate agent to identify properties within your price range.

3. Be Ready to Act Quickly: In a hot market, homes can sell quickly. Be prepared to make an offer as soon as you find a property you love. Having your finances in order and knowing what you want can help you act decisively.

4. Make a Strong Initial Offer: In competitive markets, lowball offers are often dismissed. Consider making a strong initial offer that reflects the market value of the property and shows the seller that you are serious.

5. Include an Escalation Clause: An escalation clause in your offer indicates that you are willing to increase your bid by a certain amount if another higher offer is received. This can help you stay competitive without initially offering more than necessary.

6. Limit Contingencies: While contingencies protect you, they can also make your offer less attractive to sellers. Work with your agent to determine which contingencies are essential and which can be waived or minimized to strengthen your offer.

7. Personalize Your Offer: Sometimes, a personal touch can make a difference. Consider writing a letter to the seller explaining why you love the home and how you envision your future there. Emotional appeals can sometimes sway a seller in your favor.

Financial Planning for First-Time Homebuyers

Buying your first home is a major financial commitment. Proper planning can help you navigate this process with confidence and clarity. Here are key steps for first-time homebuyers:

1. Assess Your Financial Health: Start by evaluating your current financial situation. Review your income, savings, debt, and credit score. A healthy credit score is crucial for securing a good mortgage rate.

2. Save for a Down Payment: The size of your down payment affects your mortgage terms and monthly payments. Aim to save at least 20% of the home's purchase price to avoid private mortgage insurance (PMI), although some loans require as little as 3-5%.

3. Budget for Additional Costs: Homebuying involves more than just the purchase price. Budget for closing costs (typically 2-5% of the loan amount), moving expenses, home inspections, and potential repairs or renovations.

4. Determine Your Home Affordability: Use online calculators to estimate how much house you can afford based on your income, debts, and down payment. Aim for a mortgage payment that is no more than 25-30% of your monthly income.

5. Explore Financing Options: Research different types of mortgages, including fixed-rate, adjustable-rate, FHA, VA, and

USDA loans. Each has its own eligibility requirements and benefits. Consult with a mortgage advisor to find the best option for your situation.

6. Get Pre-Approved: Pre-approval gives you a clear idea of how much you can borrow and demonstrates to sellers that you are a serious buyer. It involves submitting financial documents to a lender, who will evaluate your creditworthiness.

7. Plan for Future Expenses: Homeownership comes with ongoing costs such as property taxes, insurance, maintenance, and utilities. Create a budget that accounts for these expenses to avoid financial surprises.

Mortgage Basics and Helpful Planning Tools

Understanding the basics of mortgages is essential for making informed decisions. Here's a breakdown of key mortgage concepts and tools to assist you:

1. Types of Mortgages:

- **Fixed-Rate Mortgage:** The interest rate remains the same throughout the loan term, providing predictable monthly payments.

- **Adjustable-Rate Mortgage (ARM):** The interest rate can change periodically, typically starting lower than fixed rates but potentially increasing over time.

- **FHA Loan:** Insured by the Federal Housing Administration, ideal for first-time buyers with lower credit scores or smaller down payments.

- **VA Loan:** Available to veterans and active military members, offering favorable terms and no down payment.

- **USDA Loan:** For rural property buyers with low to moderate incomes, featuring no down payment and competitive rates.

2. Key Mortgage Terms:

- **Principal:** The loan amount borrowed to buy the home.

- **Interest Rate:** The cost of borrowing the principal, expressed as a percentage.

- **Amortization:** The process of paying off the loan through regular payments over the loan term.

- **Private Mortgage Insurance (PMI):** Required for down payments less than 20%, protecting the lender if the borrower defaults.

3. Mortgage Application Process:

- **Pre-Approval:** Submit financial documents for preliminary approval, determining how much you can borrow.

- **Home Appraisal:** An independent assessment of the home's value, required by lenders to ensure the property's worth matches the loan amount.

- **Loan Underwriting:** The lender reviews your financial information and the home appraisal to approve or deny the loan.

- **Closing:** Finalize the loan and purchase, sign documents, and pay closing costs. Ownership is transferred to you.

4. Helpful Planning Tools:

- **Mortgage Calculator:** Estimate your monthly mortgage payments, including principal, interest, taxes, and insurance (PITI).

- **Affordability Calculator:** Determine how much house you can afford based on your income, debt, and down payment.

- **Amortization Schedule:** Visualize how your mortgage payments are applied to the principal and interest over the loan term.

- **Credit Score Tracker:** Monitor and improve your credit score, a critical factor in securing favorable mortgage rates.

Conclusion

Navigating the homebuying process can be challenging, but with careful financial planning, understanding of mortgage basics, and strategies for dealing with competitive markets, you can make informed decisions and achieve your homeownership goals. Whether you're a first-time buyer or looking to invest in a new property, these tips and tools will help you approach the process with confidence and clarity.

Chapter 11: Staying Healthy During Transitions

Introduction

Moving to a new home, whether across town or across the country, can be one of the most stressful life events. Amid the excitement of new beginnings, it's easy to feel overwhelmed by the logistics and emotional strain of leaving familiar surroundings behind. This chapter aims to provide you with empathetic guidance on maintaining your health and well-being during this significant transition, offering practical tips, resources for mental health and stress management, and insights into community support systems that can help you feel at home in your new environment.

Tips on Maintaining Health and Well-Being During a Move

1. Prioritize Self-Care: Moving can be physically and emotionally taxing. Ensure you're taking care of yourself by:

- **Staying Hydrated:** Drink plenty of water to stay hydrated, especially during the physically demanding days of packing and moving.

- **Eating Nutritious Meals:** Avoid the temptation of fast food by preparing healthy meals in advance or choosing nutritious options. Simple, balanced meals can help maintain your energy levels and mood.

- **Getting Enough Sleep:** Aim for 7-9 hours of sleep each night. Adequate rest is crucial for managing stress and maintaining physical health.

2. Plan and Organize: A well-organized move can significantly reduce stress:

- **Create a Moving Checklist:** Outline all the tasks that need to be done, from packing to setting up utilities in your new home. Break the tasks into manageable steps and tackle them one at a time.

- **Pack Early:** Start packing well in advance to avoid last-minute chaos. Label boxes clearly and keep essentials accessible.

- **Hire Help if Needed:** Consider hiring professional movers or asking friends and family for assistance. Don't hesitate to delegate tasks to lighten your load.

3. Stay Physically Active: Physical activity can help reduce stress and boost your mood:

- **Take Breaks for Exercise:** Incorporate short breaks for stretching, walking, or even a quick workout. Exercise can help relieve tension and keep you energized.

- **Explore Your New Neighborhood:** Once you've moved, take walks around your new area to familiarize yourself with the surroundings and get some fresh air.

4. Maintain Social Connections: Stay connected with friends and family to feel supported during the transition:

- **Keep in Touch:** Use phone calls, video chats, and social media to stay connected with loved ones. Sharing your experiences can provide emotional support.

- **Meet New People:** Join local clubs, community groups, or social events to meet new neighbors and build a support network in your new community.

Resources for Mental Health and Stress Management

1. Professional Support: Seeking professional help can be beneficial for managing stress and mental health during a move:

- **Therapists and Counselors:** Consider talking to a therapist or counselor who can provide strategies for coping with stress and anxiety. Many offer virtual sessions, making it easier to access support.

- **Employee Assistance Programs (EAP):** If your employer offers an EAP, take advantage of the mental health resources and counseling services available to you.

2. Mindfulness and Relaxation Techniques: Incorporate mindfulness practices into your routine to manage stress:

- **Meditation:** Practice meditation to calm your mind and reduce anxiety. Apps like Headspace and Calm offer guided meditations that are easy to follow.

- **Deep Breathing Exercises:** Simple deep breathing exercises can help you relax and manage stress in the moment. Practice deep breathing by inhaling slowly through your nose, holding your breath for a few seconds, and then exhaling slowly through your mouth.

3. Self-Help Resources: Utilize self-help resources to support your mental health:

- **Books and Podcasts:** There are numerous books and podcasts on managing stress, mindfulness, and resilience that can provide valuable insights and strategies.

- **Online Communities:** Join online forums and support groups where you can share your experiences and receive encouragement from others going through similar transitions.

Community Support Systems

1. Local Support Networks: Engaging with local support networks can help you feel connected and supported in your new community:

- **Community Centers:** Visit local community centers to learn about events, classes, and groups that can help you integrate into the community.
- **Neighborhood Associations:** Join your neighborhood association to stay informed about local issues and meet your neighbors.

2. Volunteer Opportunities: Volunteering can be a great way to meet new people and give back to your community:

- **Local Charities and Nonprofits:** Explore volunteer opportunities with local charities, nonprofits, and community organizations. Volunteering can provide a sense of purpose and help you establish connections in your new town.

- **School and Youth Programs:** If you have children, consider getting involved in their school or extracurricular activities. This can help both you and your children build relationships in the community.

3. Religious and Spiritual Groups: If you have a religious or spiritual practice, connecting with a local group can provide emotional and social support:

- **Churches, Synagogues, and Mosques:** Attend services and events at local places of worship to meet others who share your faith and values.

- **Spiritual Retreats and Workshops:** Participate in retreats and workshops that focus on spiritual growth and community building.

Conclusion

Transitioning to a new home is a significant life event that can bring both excitement and stress. By prioritizing self-care, staying organized, and utilizing available resources, you can navigate this period with resilience and positivity. Remember that maintaining your mental and physical health is crucial during this time. Engage with your new community, seek support when needed, and embrace the opportunities for growth and connection that come with this transition. With the right strategies and support systems in place, you can make your new house a home and thrive in your new environment.

Appendices:

Introduction

Moving to a new area can be overwhelming, but having quick reference guides and essential information at your fingertips can make the transition smoother. This appendix provides detailed and expansive resources specific to Pittsboro, Sanford, Carthage, Siler City, and Asheboro. You'll find important contacts, utility setup instructions, annual event calendars, and a local government and service directory for each town.

Quick Reference Guides: Important Contacts, Utility Setup, and More

Pittsboro

Important Contacts:

- **Emergency Services:**
    - Police Department: (919) 542-3200
    - Fire Department: (919) 542-4101
    - EMS: (919) 542-7331
- **Healthcare:**
    - Chatham Hospital: (919) 799-4000
    - Pittsboro Family Medicine: (919) 545-0911

- **Education:**
    - Chatham County Schools: (919) 542-3626
- **City Hall:** (919) 542-4621

Utility Setup:

- **Electricity:** Duke Energy - (800) 777-9898
- **Water/Sewer:** Town of Pittsboro Utilities - (919) 542-4621
- **Gas:** PSNC Energy - (877) 776-2427
- **Trash Collection:** GFL Environmental - (919) 703-9999
- **Internet/Cable:** Spectrum - (833) 267-6094

Sanford

Important Contacts:

- **Emergency Services:**
    - Police Department: (919) 775-8268
    - Fire Department: (919) 775-8310
    - EMS: (919) 718-4620
- **Healthcare:**
    - Central Carolina Hospital: (919) 774-2100

- Sanford Health & Wellness: (919) 775-5800

- **Education:**
    - Lee County Schools: (919) 774-6226

- **City Hall:** (919) 777-1110

Utility Setup:

- **Electricity:** Duke Energy - (800) 777-9898

- **Water/Sewer:** City of Sanford Utilities - (919) 775-8211

- **Gas:** Piedmont Natural Gas - (800) 752-7504

- **Trash Collection:** City of Sanford Public Works - (919) 775-8312

- **Internet/Cable:** Spectrum - (833) 267-6094

Carthage

Important Contacts:

- **Emergency Services:**
    - Police Department: (910) 947-2231
    - Fire Department: (910) 947-2151
    - EMS: (910) 947-6370

- **Healthcare:**

- FirstHealth Moore Regional Hospital - Carthage: (910) 947-3000
- Carthage Family Medicine: (910) 947-3000

- **Education:**
  - Moore County Schools: (910) 947-2976

- **Town Hall:** (910) 947-2331

Utility Setup:

- **Electricity:** Duke Energy - (800) 777-9898
- **Water/Sewer:** Town of Carthage Utilities - (910) 947-2331
- **Gas:** Piedmont Natural Gas - (800) 752-7504
- **Trash Collection:** Town of Carthage Public Works - (910) 947-2331
- **Internet/Cable:** Spectrum - (833) 267-6094

Siler City

Important Contacts:

- **Emergency Services:**
  - Police Department: (919) 742-5626

- Fire Department: (919) 742-5731
- EMS: (919) 742-4550

- **Healthcare:**
    - Chatham Hospital: (919) 799-4000
    - Siler City Community Health Center: (919) 663-1744

- **Education:**
    - Chatham County Schools: (919) 542-3626

- **Town Hall:** (919) 742-4731

Utility Setup:

- **Electricity:** Duke Energy - (800) 777-9898
- **Water/Sewer:** Town of Siler City Utilities - (919) 742-4731
- **Gas:** Piedmont Natural Gas - (800) 752-7504
- **Trash Collection:** Town of Siler City Public Works - (919) 742-5731
- **Internet/Cable:** Spectrum - (833) 267-6094

Asheboro

Important Contacts:

- **Emergency Services:**
    - Police Department: (336) 626-1300
    - Fire Department: (336) 626-1201
    - EMS: (336) 625-5000
- **Healthcare:**
    - Randolph Health: (336) 625-5151
    - Asheboro Family Physicians: (336) 625-4261
- **Education:**
    - Asheboro City Schools: (336) 625-5104
- **City Hall:** (336) 626-1201

Utility Setup:

- **Electricity:** Duke Energy - (800) 777-9898
- **Water/Sewer:** City of Asheboro Utilities - (336) 626-1201
- **Gas:** Piedmont Natural Gas - (800) 752-7504
- **Trash Collection:** City of Asheboro Public Works - (336) 626-1234

- **Internet/Cable:** Spectrum - (833) 267-6094

Annual Events Calendar for Each Town

Pittsboro

- **First Sunday Artisan Fair:** Monthly event showcasing local crafts, food, and live music.
- **Pittsboro Street Fair:** October event featuring local vendors, food trucks, and entertainment.
- **Chatham County Fair:** Annual event in September with rides, games, and agricultural exhibits.
- **Holiday Parade:** December parade celebrating the holiday season with floats, bands, and Santa Claus.

Sanford

- **Sanford Arts & Vine Festival:** April event celebrating local art, wine, and crafts.
- **Depot Park Concert Series:** Summer concert series featuring local and regional musicians.
- **Sanford Pottery Festival:** November event showcasing pottery and crafts from local artisans.
- **Christmas in the Park:** December event with holiday lights, music, and festivities in Depot Park.

Carthage

- **Carthage Buggy Festival:** May festival celebrating the town's buggy-making history with parades, music, and vendors.

- **Hillcrest Park Summer Concerts:** Summer concert series with live music and family activities.

- **Carthage Fall Festival:** October event featuring crafts, food vendors, and live entertainment.

- **Christmas Tree Lighting:** December event with carol singing, hot cocoa, and tree lighting in the town square.

Siler City

- **Siler City Latino Festival:** May celebration of Latino culture with music, dance, and food.

- **Third Friday Art Walk:** Monthly event featuring local art galleries, live music, and street vendors.

- **Harvest Festival:** October event with crafts, food, and family activities in downtown Siler City.

- **Holiday Parade:** December parade with floats, bands, and community groups celebrating the holiday season.

Asheboro

- **North Carolina Zoo Events:** Year-round events at the zoo, including Boo at the Zoo (October) and ZooFest (June).

- **Bicentennial Park Summer Concerts:** Summer concert series with local and regional musicians.

- **Fall Festival:** October event with crafts, food, and entertainment in downtown Asheboro.

- **Christmas on Sunset:** December event featuring holiday lights, music, and shopping in downtown Asheboro.

Local Government and Service Directory

Pittsboro

- **Mayor's Office:** (919) 542-4621

- **Town Manager:** (919) 542-4621

- **Building Permits:** (919) 542-4621

- **Public Works:** (919) 542-4621

- **Parks and Recreation:** (919) 542-4621

Sanford

- **Mayor's Office:** (919) 777-1110
- **City Manager:** (919) 777-1110
- **Building Permits:** (919) 777-1122
- **Public Works:** (919) 775-8211
- **Parks and Recreation:** (919) 775-8242

Carthage

- **Mayor's Office:** (910) 947-2331
- **Town Manager:** (910) 947-2331
- **Building Permits:** (910) 947-2331
- **Public Works:** (910) 947-2331
- **Parks and Recreation:** (910) 947-2331

Siler City

- **Mayor's Office:** (919) 742-4731
- **Town Manager:** (919) 742-4731
- **Building Permits:** (919) 742-4731
- **Public Works:** (919) 742-4731
- **Parks and Recreation:** (919) 742-2699

Asheboro

- **Mayor's Office:** (336) 626-1201
- **City Manager:** (336) 626-1201
- **Building Permits:** (336) 626-1201
- **Public Works:** (336) 626-1201
- **Parks and Recreation:** (336) 626-1240

Conclusion

These appendices provide a comprehensive overview of the essential resources available in Pittsboro, Sanford, Carthage, Siler City, and Asheboro. From setting up utilities to finding important contacts and understanding local government services, this information will help you settle into your new community with ease. Additionally, the annual events calendars highlight the vibrant cultural life in these towns, ensuring that you have ample opportunities to engage with your new neighbors and enjoy the unique offerings of each area. Whether you're moving to one of these towns or just visiting, these resources will guide you in making the most of your time in North Carolina's Historic Heartlands.

About the Author

Crystal Hutchinson is a passionate real estate broker and motivational writer based in Raleigh, North Carolina. With a rich background in law and a deep enthusiasm for helping people, Crystal transitioned from a successful legal career to real estate after moving to Raleigh in 2022. Her extensive experience as an attorney has equipped her with exceptional negotiation skills and a keen eye for detail, making her an invaluable asset in the real estate market.

Dedicated to helping clients navigate the real estate market with confidence and ease, Crystal provides expert guidance whether you are buying or selling a home in North Carolina or seeking advice on relocation. Her comprehensive understanding of the market, combined with her personalized approach, ensures that every client feels supported and well-informed throughout the process.

Crystal's commitment to client satisfaction extends beyond North Carolina. With referral partners in every state, she can connect you with top-notch agents no matter where you have a home to sell. Her extensive network guarantees that you will receive the best service and support, regardless of your location.

Connect with Crystal Hutchinson:

- **Email:** crystalsellsnchomes@gmail.com
- **YouTube Channel:** Real NC Living With Crystal
- **Facebook:** Living in NC with Crystal
- **Instagram:** RealNCLiving_Crystal
- **TikTok:** RealNCLiving_Crystal

Crystal Hutchinson is here to help you achieve your real estate dreams. Reach out today to start your journey with a dedicated and knowledgeable partner by your side.

References

1. North Carolina Department of Public Instruction. (n.d.). School Performance Data. Retrieved from www.ncpublicschools.org.

2. GreatSchools. (n.d.). School Ratings and Reviews. Retrieved from www.greatschools.org.

3. U.S. Department of Education. (n.d.). National Center for Education Statistics. Retrieved from nces.ed.gov.

4. North Carolina GreenTravel Initiative. (n.d.). Sustainable Tourism Practices. Retrieved from www.ncgreentravel.org.

5. Spectrum. (n.d.). Internet and Cable Services. Retrieved from www.spectrum.com.

6. Duke Energy. (n.d.). Utility Services. Retrieved from www.duke-energy.com.

7. PSNC Energy. (n.d.). Natural Gas Services. Retrieved from www.psncenergy.com.

8. FirstHealth of the Carolinas. (n.d.). Healthcare Services. Retrieved from www.firsthealth.org.

9. Piedmont Health Services. (n.d.). Community Health Services. Retrieved from www.piedmonthealth.org.

10. Chatham Park. (n.d.). Community Development and Employment Opportunities. Retrieved from www.chathampark.com.

www.ingramcontent.com/pod-product-compliance
Lightning Source LLC
Chambersburg PA
CBHW070110230526
45472CB00004B/1208